DON'T LET THEM STEAL YOUR BRAND

11 Vacation Rental Niches to Make Your Bookings Soar

BY DEBORAH S. NELSON

Author-Speaker-Publisher
The Vacation Rental Travel Guide

Copyright © 2018 by Deborah S. Nelson.

ISBN-13: 978-1977791023
ISBN-10: 1977791026

The author retains sole copyright to her contributions to this book.
Cover design by Sara Winner.

The interactive goal setting teaching model introduced in this series is patent pending; and may not be used without permission or a licensing agreement from DS Publishing Company.

Published by DS Publishing Company 3107 W Colorado Ave #303 Colorado Springs CO 80904

All Rights Reserved

No part of this book may be reproduced or used in any form without permission from the publisher. The original purchaser is hereby granted permission to print pages for personal use.

Copies of this may NOT be transmitted, stored, or recorded in any form without written permission from the publisher, DS Publishing Company, will prosecute any violations of copyright law, including e-mail attachments or any other means.

DEDICATION

This book is dedicated to Sidney Berger, whose grand and generous support of Lauren and the Lauren Berger Collection has allowed her to touch thousands in the vacation rental industry.

Lauren has inspired, supported and mentored me in this spectacular industry. I continually strive to match her upscale excellence, hospitality, and perfectionism.

Without Sidney's loving support of Lauren the vacation rental industry would not be where it is today. Maybe God be with him.

FREE BONUS
BRANDING BOMBS

http://www.thevacationrentalguide.com/landingpage/branding-mula/

BRANDING TOOLS WORKSHOP

http://www.thevacationrentalguide.com/workshop-schedule/

INTRODUCTION

This book will teach you about the DNA of the Vacation Rental Guest and how to engage them through the vehicle of niche branding. Ultimately, an engaged prospect is a booked guest—and that's the big idea!

Let's get started: I want to let you know that I applaud you for investing this time in your education; and for taking time to read this book. YAY, YOU! So, what do I know? How can I help you to increase your bottom line?

I will answer those questions, but first—my name is Deborah Nelson and I am the Publisher of The Vacation Rental Travel Guide. The Vacation Rental Travel Guide is a series on AMAZON INTERNATIONAL and also Online in an animated flip version.

We offer the traveler powerful information leading them to embrace the vacation rental travel experience—while also creating visibility, credibility, and

INTRODUCTION

publicity for niche-related vacation rental properties.

The vacation rental business has been good to us. It granted us the extra income needed for my daughter's final year of college and gave me a new career—publishing and consulting in the vacation rental Industry. Along the way, I managed, branded, and booked six vacation rentals for years.

Now, I have published seven vacation rental books. I also do vacation rental consulting and have helped property owners to start their successful vacation rental ventures. So, I think and hope I can help you.

TABLE OF CONTENTS

My Mission	1
We've Got Your Number	3
The Vacation Rental Story	5
Numbers, Numbers, Numbers	9
The Most Important Numbers Today	11
History of Vacation Rentals	15
Guest DNA Wants	19
From Numbers to Niches	21
Find Your Niche	25
Definition of Niche Branding	26
Sample of Niche Branding Flyer	27
Build Your Brand	29
Niche 1: Beach Area Vacation Rentals	33
Brainstorming: Beach Area Niche	35
Niche 2: Family Focused Vacation Rentals	39
Brainstorming: Family Focused Niche	41
Niche 3: Outstandingly Located Vacation Rentals	45
Brainstorming: Outstandingly Located Niche	47
Niche 4: Retreat & Event Vacation Rentals	51
Brainstorming: Retreat & Event Niche	53
Niche 5: Super Romantic Vacation Rentals	57

TABLE OF CONTENTS

Brainstorming: Super Romantic Niche	59
Niche 6: Ultra Luxurious Vacation Rentals	63
Brainstorming: Ultra Luxurious Niche	65
Niche 7: Unusually Unique Vacation Rentals	69
Brainstorming: Unusually Unique Niche	71
Niche 8: Vacation Rentals for the Sports Enthusiast	75
Brainstorming: Sports Enthusiast Niche	77
Niche 9: Vacation Rentals for Wine Lovers	81
Brainstorming: Wine Lover Niche	83
Niche 10: Value Conscious Vacation Rentals	87
Brainstorming: Value Conscious Niche	89
Niche 11: Pet Friendly Vacation Rentals	93
Brainstorming: Pet Friendly Niche	95
Niche 12: Your Vacation Rental Niche	99
Brainstorming: Your Vacation Rental Niche	101
Summary	105

MY MISSION

My mission with this book is to motivate, inspire, teach, and to give you an edge in this industry. I want you to learn how to leverage tools that will increase your booking numbers—and percentage of inquiries booked, so you spend less time talking and more time booking. But how are we going to accomplish this?

First off, we are going to talk about your *number*, and some other important numbers. Secondly, we will explore the DNA of the vacation rental guest. Then we will make the shift from Numbers to Niches—lastly, we will do a brainstorming session to Define Your Niche and how to Apply Your Niche—all this for the purpose of increasing YOUR NUMBER.

Now I know what you might be thinking ... DNA, NUMBERS & NICHES, how is that going to help me? But trust me—I am going to connect the dots for you step by step.

WE'VE GOT YOUR NUMBER

To get started right away, I want you to write down a number between 10-25%. This number will represent the increase in your bookings for the remainder of this year.

If you have been around a while and manage a number of vacation properties, a 10% increase is significant. If you are new and still building a client base, a bigger number is appropriate.

Get out a piece of paper or write this number in your cell phone. I want you to think about what that number can mean to you or write it here_____.

A 15% increase may mean a new car to some of you, or it might mean the ability to pay off that pesky old credit card debt once and for all. For others it could mean the ability to take a vacation, or maybe just buy a vacation rental home of your own. Just get that number on a piece of paper right now and I'll tell you more later on.

VACATION RENTALS
NEXT EXIT ↗

MY VACATION RENTAL STORY

I came into this industry quite by happy accident. When sending my daughter on an independent study in college, I needed to find a solution for making three monthly housing payments—practically impossible, I thought.

Then, I bumped into a creative solution—and rented my town home in Colorado short term. I stayed in my daughter's college apartment in Santa Barbara, while she lived in Europe for 2 months. When she returned from Europe, I was invited stay in Santa Barbara with an offer I could not refuse.

Meanwhile, I had listed the Colorado condo on VRBO, and Wa Laa! My journey in the vacation rental business had begun.

The vacation rental business has been good to us. It granted us the extra income needed for my daughter's final year of college and granted me a new career—publishing and consulting in the vacation rental Industry. Along the way, I managed, branded, and booked six vacation rentals for years.

MY VACATION RENTAL STORY

Presently, I have published seven vacation rental books. I also do vacation rental consulting and have helped property owners to start their successful vacation rental ventures. So, I think and hope I can help you.

This industry is near and dear to my heart but it is also tumultuous. The vacation rental industry is going through a lot of growing pains right now.

I remember in 2009 after being in the industry for four years when everything started to foreclose; and all of a sudden, a flood of amateurs entered the market. They were not charging cleaning fees, and under bidding the rest of us like crazy! And that is when I shifted from vacation rental management to writing vacation rental books.

NUMBERS, NUMBERS, NUMBERS

You have invested some numbers yourself—the time that it takes to read the book. My goal today, is to help you gain a new inspiration and ... a new number and a new niche.

We talk a lot about numbers in this industry—how many days, how many bedrooms, bathrooms, how many people, how much does it cost?

These numbers represent guest needs; and guests need the answers to these questions. The OTA's perform well with their high-tech search engines answering those questions and bringing the inquiries to you.

But once we get the inquiry, how are we going to close more bookings—how are we going to bring these guests back ... and if not these guests, how are we going to bring their friends and relatives to visit? How are we going to close more bookings from the inquiries we receive?

NUMBERS, NUMBERS, NUMBERS

My advice is this. Take the shift ... the shift from NUMBERS to NICHES.

Try it for one or more of your newer properties. Before we do that let's look at some very important numbers; and then next, a little history lesson.

THE MOST IMPORTANT NUMBERS TODAY

Tripping.com is an aggregator site with about 8 million listings from the top vacation rental listing companies. The following chart includes the "fee information" for all the top sites. These are some important numbers we might consider in deciding where to list our properties.

In making the shift from numbers to niches, our job as property managers is to brand in order to book properties. We strive to provide niche-related hospitality to guests to keep them coming back—AND referring our brand to friends and family. If you will notice on this list of vacation rental listing sites, only a few are still free to guests to book—just one of the ways the numbers in this industry are under constant change.

THE MOST IMPORTANT NUMBERS TODAY

	Listing Fees
Find Rentals	$36 per property per year
VRBO (Vacation Rentals By Owner)	Annual Subscription: $349
Luxury Retreats	Free
VacationRentals	Annual Subscription: $399
FlipKey by TripAdvisor	FlipKey hosts can list for free.
HomeAway	Annual Subscription: $399
Airbnb	No Annual Subscription
Way to Stay	Free
CanadaStays	Annual Subscription: $349 (Canadian Dollars)

DON'T LET THEM STEAL YOUR BRAND

Pay-Per-Booking	Guest Fees
No booking fees; Find Rentals allows guests to book direct through the vacation rental managers.	Free
Pay nothing upfront, than pay a minimum of 8% on each booking	Ranges between 12%-15%
Free	Ranges between 5%-15%
Pay nothing upfront, than pay a minimum of 8% on each booking	Ranges between 5%-12%
3%	Ranges between 5%-15%
Pay nothing upfront, than pay a minimum of 8% on each booking	Ranges between 4%-10%
3%	Ranges between 5%-15%
Free	Free
10%	8%

HISTORY OF VACATION RENTALS

Before the Internet, vacation rentals were primarily a mom-and-pop industry—and organically popular in Europe. Businesses advertised via classifieds or real estate agents; some mailed promotions to travel-related lists. With the Internet, like for most industries, came significant changes.

A Colorado couple looking for a better way to rent their ski condo launched Vacation Rental By Owner in 1996—otherwise known as VRBO. Ten years later, Home Away acquired the business in 2006, along with many others, creating a semi-monopoly, and became the dominant listings hub. Then last year, Expedia devoured Home Away, paying $3.9 billion for the purchase.

Today, the Expedia-HomeAway combo moves ahead of Booking.com as the world's largest accommodations site. Expedia Inc. now offers an estimated 1.3 million properties—compared with Booking.com's 821,400.

HISTORY OF VACATION RENTALS

The Future & More Numbers

The 1996 cottage industry has evolved into a major corporate endeavor. The industry is said to be worth $100 billion, with the United States accounting for about 25% of that—about 24 billion per year. Estimates show that the current $100 billion-dollar market is on track to grow to nearly $170 billion by 2019 and to $285 billion by 2025.

Meanwhile, Skift, an Online business stats service, calculates that in the first four months of 2016 alone, vacation rentals startups attracted nearly $100 million in venture capital funding.

Yesterday, the vacation rental industry was an Internet experiment. Today, with these numbers, it's a whole new story! Think of the opportunity. Those who adjust and adapt to the changes, will be successful in taking vacation property management to its highest level.

With the industry focused on numbers and approximately 8 million listings, at VRTG, we believe that booking behavior is going to shift and in fact it already has. In the United States, the percentage of adults who have stayed in a vacation rental has quadrupled from eight percent in 2011 to 32 percent in 2015.

One natural reason that travelers have gravitated towards vacation rentals instead of hotels is because they offer the unique and the exciting unknown, along with the human desire to book a comfortable home instead. Many value this option over a predictable beige corporate hotel, located near a stereotypical Denny's or Seven Eleven. They are looking for a little something more.

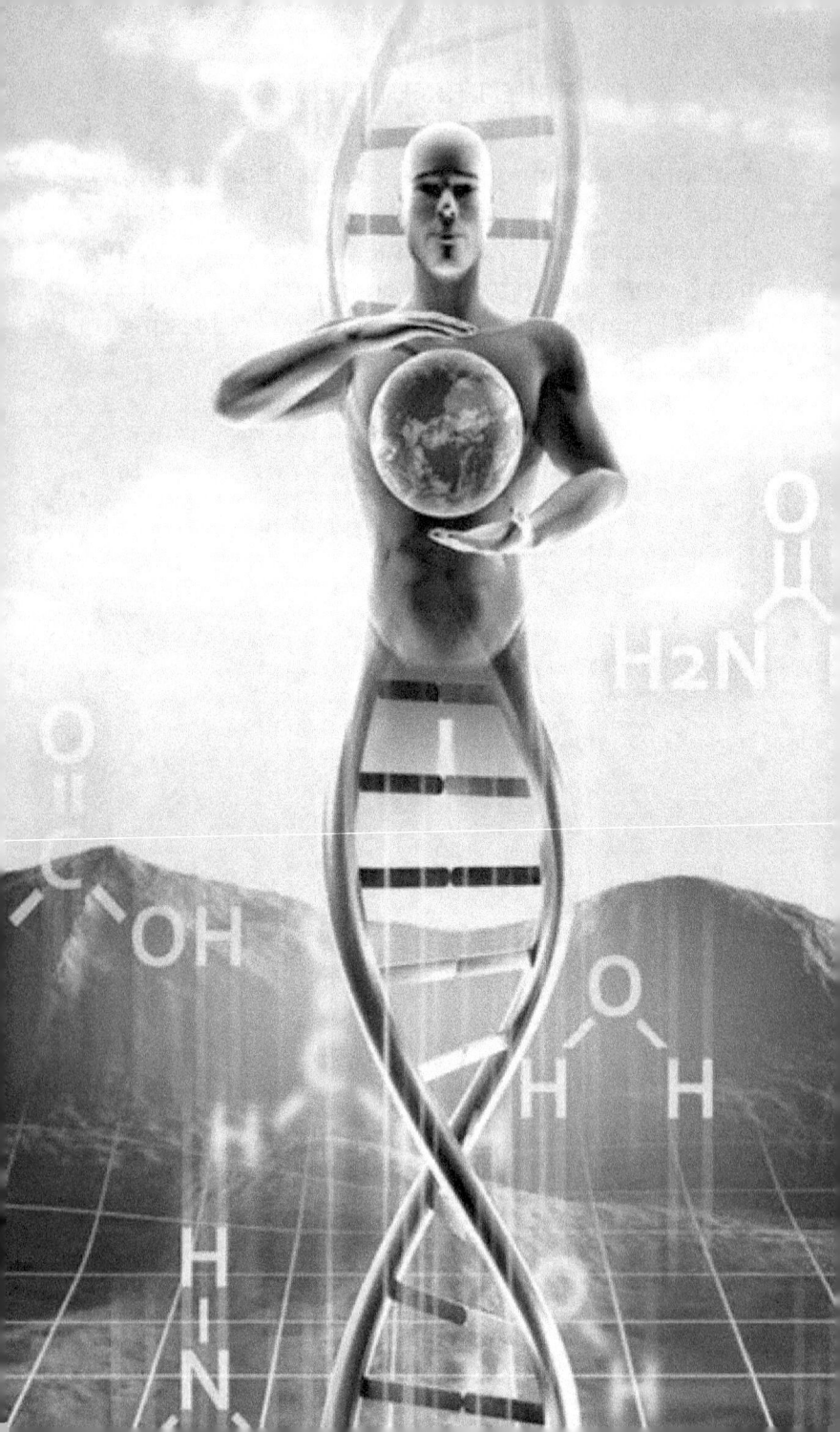

GUEST DNA WANTS

1. Rest, fun, adventure
2. Escape from reality
3. Spend quality time with family
4. A place and time for romance
5. Privacy and Anonymity

When we talk about the DNA of the Vacation Rental Traveler, we strive to understand both their needs and their wants. Their needs are about the numbers, and wants are about the desires of their heart. Actually, engaging their deeper wants and desires involves selecting and creating an attractive niche brand.

↑ **YOUR NICHE** ↑

FROM NUMBERS TO NICHES

Two main emotions motivate a sale, or in our world—a booking. The first is needs; the second is wants. The needs of a vacation rental guest includes numbers—how many bedrooms, bathrooms, how many people, how many days, how much cost, etc. The OTA's do a good job sending over guest inquiries based on the numbers. But most, let's remember that most vacation rental guests want to be treated like human beings—NOT a number!

And so back to YOUR NUMBER that you wrote down. To see YOUR NUMBER increase, consider your guests' wants. Once their number needs are met, you may use a niche to fulfill the wants of the guest. Stimulating and answering wants can inspire a quick booking decision.

Meeting our travelers with a niche brand allows us to touch their wants quickly as they make their decision among the many alternatives. For example, your place is near one of the top mountain golf courses in the country, or three miles from DISNEY WORLD.

These might seem like obvious advantages, but once you identify a niche, and align your brand identity with that niche, you can more easily close the sale by addressing the wants and desires of that guest. But how do you learn what those wants and desires are?

Let's brainstorm your potential niche by examining why guests might book your property:

TYPE OF PEOPLE: What types of people have booked your property so far? Are they family focused? Are they single surfers, Yoga enthusiasts, older couples? What is the common thread of the people who have already booked your spot?

LOCALITY: Is your geographic area near water, mountains, and family theme parks? What is primarily bringing travelers to your vacation home's locale?

SPECIAL EXPERTISE: Is there an interest such as hang gliding, kite surfing, helicopter rides, or other popular interest in your area--an area expert that is known worldwide? Maybe it's a cooking school, or a language institute, or a training center. Examine where your property might overlap with what these types of guest might value about your vacation rental spot.

By the end of this book you will identify a niche, and understand how to address the wants and desires and hopes of your traveling guest.

DON'T LET THEM STEAL YOUR BRAND

NOTES:

_____

_____

_____

_____

_____

_____

_____

_____

_____

_____

_____

_____

_____

_____

_____

FIND YOUR NICHE

Before you finish reading, I want you to have defined your niche. Then, also identify one or two ways to begin to brand your property to that niche as well as how to reach potential travelers in that niche. These four segments may help you find an ideal niche:

- Niche related to your area: certain tourist attractions, geographic feature

- Niche related to your vacation rental structure, design, or grounds

- Niche related to an interest: golfing, scuba diving, surfing, which enjoys superior venues for these in your area.

- Niche related to events: sports event, Broadway events, film festivals, etc.

DEFINITION OF NICHE BRANDING

Definition of Niche Marketing: Concentrating all marketing efforts on a small but specific and well-defined segment of the population. Niches do not 'exist' but are 'created' by identifying needs, wants, and requirements that are being addressed poorly or not at all by other firms, and developing and delivering goods or services to satisfy them. As a strategy, niche marketing is aimed at being a big fish in a small pond instead of being a small fish in a big pond—also called micro-marketing.

- *The Business Dictionary*

Sample of a logo for niche branding

DON'T LET THEM STEAL YOUR BRAND

SAMPLE OF NICHE BRANDING FLYER

This is one of the brands I helped to create for a client with a Penthouse by the Beach in the Dominican Republic. Niche branding can start simply and move into more sophistication. Start with a name, a logo, and a flyer.

BUILD YOUR
BRAND

BUILD YOUR BRAND

The ability to niche brand anything has never been easier than as it is today. The concept of niche branding is simply building a relationship with a subset of people who love what you do, sell, or provide.

A good example of this is to look at the growth of cable TV channels. A few years ago, we did not have access to a golf channel, NFL, or even an entire channel dedicated to gardening. Start building your brand with the following steps:

1. **Brand Name**

   Create a brand name for each vacation rental property based on a niche (you might want to experiment with one property, first). Some of you have done this, but many are using unit numbers and the name of the development. Take it further! Use the niche to develop a brand name for each vacation property. Consider your guests perspective when naming your vacation rental properties. Gear your brand name towards the desires of traveler. Try to think the way they do, when creating a name.

2. Reach Your Niche

An intriguing brand name for you niche is one thing, but telling the world about it is another! You can start with your website—building rapport with your visitors by giving them access to quality information about your niche. You can start by telling everything there is to know about your niche—benefits, how it works, how useful it is to their daily life, and so on.

Send articles around to various sites and join social networking sites to gather interested contacts to become a part of your niche database. Start a mailing list to spread and share your niche info. Build your own guest list separate from the OTA's in order to reach out for those repeat visits, referrals, and great reviews.

Another idea is to team up with affiliate marketers, travel agents, or related niche venues to market your niche—especially locals. The more people representing your niche in the field, the more potential guests will be exposed to your vacation properties.

3. **Build Solid Guest Relationships to Keep Them Coming Back**

When I worked in the branding industry and created imprinted merchandise we knew that the most inexpensive customer is the one you already have.

DON'T LET THEM STEAL YOUR BRAND

Using a niche brand helps to nurture the guests and travelers who already know us. This is where you can invite them to return or make a referral.

If you noticed on the charts from Tripping.com, fees paid to the listing site can be up to 15%. So, offering your guest a 10% discount next time they book, or for friends and family, who directly book from you, brings guests back at a fraction of the cost. A repeat or referral guest is the easiest and least expensive way to fill your vacancies.

Once they arrive, put niche hospitality into place. Build a personal relationship with guests by giving a thorough walk through, offering concierge services, and creating a WELCOME MANUAL with local brochures, maps, even discount coupons in niche related enterprises. The discount can attract more guests from the same niche. Niches tend to be tight circles and over time the word will spread.

To achieve success in any niche depends on focus and interaction—interact with your guests.

Spend a little time talking to them about their niche. If they are interested in biking, and your neighborhood is near a biking trail, provide bikes for rent. Major on the minor—be niche conscious. Bring your niche into interior decorating, discount coupons, the grounds, and in any way, you can to promote the niche and interests of your guest.

NICHE 1: BEACH AREA VACATION RENTALS

The Vacation Rental Travel Guide has identified 11 popular travel niches, and we reach out to our travelers in their areas of interests, wants, and desires. Most of the main niches will also have sub-niches, but staying with the main niche will help you attract from a wider target audience. This first niche, Beach Area Vacation Rentals is a lot more comprehensive than the rest, so you may get the idea how you could promote your niche vacation rental.

Use the points to apply to each niche to find ways of promoting your brand: Location, area enterprises, and local events.

BRAINSTORMING: BEACH AREA NICHE

Niche 1, Beach Area Vacation Rentals: LOOKING TO GET AWAY FROM LONG, COLD, SNOWY WINTERS? DOES THE SOUND OF ROLLING SURF GIVE YOU THAT AHH FEELING?

1. <u>Beach Area Location:</u> Is your vacation rental is near well-known attractions such as Atlantic City (boardwalk); Santa Monica Pacific Park (amusement park) and Dana Point (historic surfing spot). If you vacation rental is within 10-25 miles of a major attraction consider those part of your niche brand. If properties are ocean front; within beach walking distance; or ocean view, feature these as brand talking points in promo materials & emails. Include the keywords "beach" and "beach area" within your brand name.

2. <u>Beach Area Enterprises:</u> Create a THREE RING NOTEBOOK using plastic sleeves which include local beach area restaurants, attractions, and activities. Agree to include a coupon or a brochure in your WELCOME MANUAL for key enterprises

BRAINSTORMING: BEACH AREA VACATION NICHE

in exchange for leaving flyers about your vacation rental property near their cash register, on their bulletin board, or exchanging web links.

3. <u>**Beach Events**</u>: Surfing competitions, music festivals, beach volleyball tournaments—identify beach related events that attract out of town guests. Check with local celebrities, wedding planners, and event coordinators to give them flyers with info on your vacation rentals.

4. <u>**Announce your Niche to Travel Agencies**</u>: Set up an appointment with local travel agencies for a walk-through or open house of your vacation homes. Agree to give them a commission for bookings.

5. <u>**What do you Think?**</u>

_____

_____

_____

_____

_____

_____

DON'T LET THEM STEAL YOUR BRAND

Notes:

NICHE 2: FAMILY FOCUSED VACATION RENTALS

FAMILY FOCUSED VACATION HOMES FOR FAMILIES WHO WANT A *HOME AWAY FROM HOME* WITH ACTIVITIES ON HAND FOR CHILDREN.

Most family focused homes are equipped with children's bedrooms, closets full of toys, baby furniture, and child-sized dining tables. Families can feel free to make joyful noise that isn't easily accepted in a hotel setting. Enjoy a barbecue by the pool in the private backyard of a family focused vacation rental.

BRAINSTORMING: FAMILY FOCUSED NICHE

Think about the following:

FAMILY FOCUSED LOCATION: Consider nearby family area locations such as theme parks, water parks, and local recreational centers or parks and make that a part of your niche branding.

FAMILY FOCUSED ENTERPRISES: Network with popular family restaurants, or attractions, activities and exchange promotional materials with them.

FAMILY FOCUSED EVENTS: Identify events, trainings, college orientations which attract families. For example in Colorado Springs there was the Olympic training center where families often stayed for up to a month while their kid was training. Leave flyers, exchange information, network.

TRAVEL AGENCIES: Host an open house to showcase vacation homes to travel agencies & pay them a 5-15% commission for bookings.

BRAINSTORMING: FAMILY FOCUSED NICHE

WHAT DO YOU THINK?

Notes:

DON'T LET THEM STEAL YOUR BRAND

NICHE 3: OUTSTANDINGLY LOCATED VACATION RENTALS

ARE YOU THE TYPE OF TRAVELER LESS INTERESTING IN WHERE YOU SLEEP AND MORE INTERESTED IN WHERE YOU GO?

There are so many intriguing places in the world—from Hawaii's shores to Croatia's coast for the beach lover; California's Lake Tahoe and Washington State for skiing; to New York City for theater and fine dining; to name just a few places where our VRTG reviewers have visited and written about.

BRAINSTORMING: OUTSTANDINGLY LOCATED NICHE

Think about the following:

OUTSTANDINGLY LOCATED AREAS: In outstanding locations identify the iconic attractions of the area. For example, if your outstandingly located vacation home is in Paris, include the Eiffel Tower, and other such landmarks in your branding.

OUTSTANDINGLY LOCATED ENTERPRISES: Network with the more and less popular enterprises of the area and exchange promotional materials with them.

OUTSTANDINGLY LOCATED EVENTS: Identify popular local events. For example, in New York there's a global New York Film Festival, Broadway Plays, New York Giants Games. Network with these venues. Invite them to open houses, so they can see your property and recommend them to their attendees.

TRAVEL AGENCIES: Host an open house to showcase

BRAINSTORMING: OUTSTANDINGLY LOCATED NICHE

vacation homes to travel agencies & pay them a 5-15% commission for bookings.

WHAT DO YOU THINK?

_____

_____

_____

_____

_____

_____

_____

Notes:

_____

_____

_____

_____

DON'T LET THEM STEAL YOUR BRAND

NICHE 4: RETREAT & EVENT VACATION RENTALS

RETREATS, WEDDING PARTIES, FAMILY REUNIONS, & EVENTS ARE MADE MEMORABLE BY VACATION RENTALS WELL-SUITED FOR GROUPS

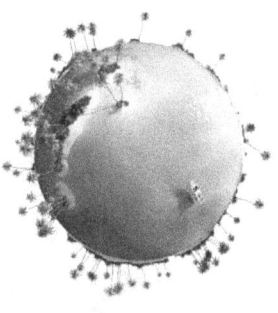

Well-equipped kitchens, spacious common areas, private bedroom suites, and a plethora of bathrooms make these rentals excellent choices. Many of the retreat and event rentals offer ample grounds with swimming pool, spa, gym, and recreational areas. Optional chefs for hire make dining run smoothly, while letting you focus on the event.

BRAINSTORMING: RETREAT & EVENT NICHE

Think about the following:

RETREAT & EVENT LOCATION: Consider networking with area churches, wedding planners, event organizers, music promoters to make your vacation rental available to them.

RETREAT & EVENT ENTERPRISES: Network with organizations who might have an interest in coming to your area. These enterprises can be local, but will also likely to be from a distance away. Think of any organization who does trainings, retreats, weddings, and any of the events which your place is ideal.

RETREAT & EVENT EVENTS: You may want to go to wedding trade shows, family reunion workshops, and event planner seminars. Network and invite anyone to open houses, your website, and further conversation.

TRAVEL AGENCIES: Host an open house to showcase

BRAINSTORMING: RETREAT & EVENT NICHE

vacation homes to travel agencies & pay them a 5-15% commission for bookings.

WHAT DO YOU THINK?

___

___

___

___

___

___

___

Notes:

___

___

___

___

___

DON'T LET THEM STEAL YOUR BRAND

NICHE 5: SUPER ROMANTIC VACATION RENTALS

LOVE IS A MANY-SPLENDORED THING; LOVE IS LIKE OXYGEN; UP WHERE WE BELONG; ALL YOU NEED IS LOVE—WONDERFUL LOVE SONGS.

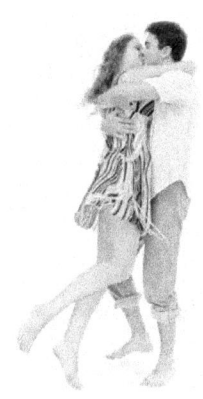

Whether you are finally reconnecting after months of a hectic schedule, renewing vows or looking to spend time away from responsibilities, vacations can be an inspired time to reawaken your romantic self.

BRAINSTORMING: SUPER ROMANTIC NICHE

Think about the following:

SUPER ROMANTIC LOCATIONS: If you are located in San Francisco, Paris, New York City, or a few other known romantic locations, take advantage of the most romantic aspects of the area and emphasize in your branding.

SUPER ROMANTIC ENTERPRISES: In New York City, An Affair to Remember with Kerry Grant, was filmed on the Empire State Building. Make the Empire State Building a part of your branding strategy—even include a pair of tickets to the Empire State Building when they book.

SUPER ROMANTIC EVENTS: Be aware of Valentines day, wedding shows, romantic plays, and connect with those around the events by inviting them to open house, or to have a virtual tour of your vacation home.

TRAVEL AGENCIES: Host an open house to showcase

BRAINSTORMING: SUPER ROMANTIC NICHE

vacation homes to travel agencies & pay them a 5-15% commission for bookings.

WHAT DO YOU THINK?

___

___

___

___

___

___

___

Notes:

___

___

___

___

DON'T LET THEM STEAL YOUR BRAND

NICHE 6: ULTRA LUXURIOUS VACATION RENTALS

A LUXURIOUS VACATION HOME IS AN INDULGENCE WHICH PROVIDES PLEASURE FOR TRAVELERS WHO SEEK AN UNFORGETTABLE TIME.

Luxurious vacation rentals offer many amenities and niceties making it possible to enjoy a fantastic vacation without leaving the property! Once you do venture forth, you will discover beautiful surroundings.

BRAINSTORMING: ULTRA LUXURIOUS NICHE

Think about the following:

ULTRA LUXURIOUS LOCATION: You may be in an ultra luxurious area, or your vacation home may be ultra luxurious. Connect with luxurious attractions such as Ships, Yachts, Castles, and attractions where people who prefer luxury frequent. Make these a part of your brand.

ULTRA LUXURIOUS ENTERPRISES: Visit high end car or yacht dealerships, boutiques, and invite them to open houses, give them flyers, or create a co-marketing strategy with them, to share clients.

ULTRA LUXURIOUS EVENTS: Seek out billionaire events, luxury trade shows, cigar or wine tasting events, for the opportunity to network with those of include in this market.

TRAVEL AGENCIES: Host an open house to showcase vacation homes to travel agencies & pay them a 5-15% commission for bookings.

BRAINSTORMING: ULTRA LUXURIOUS NICHE

WHAT DO YOU THINK?

Notes:

DON'T LET THEM STEAL YOUR BRAND

DON'T LET THEM STEAL YOUR BRAND

NICHE 7: UNUSUALLY UNIQUE VACATION RENTALS

YOU ARE NOT ONE TO ENGAGE IN THE ORDINARY. AS A CREATIVE PERSON, YOU NEED THE EXCITEMENT OF THE UNIQUE AND UNUSUAL.

VRTG brings you both unusual and unique in vacation rentals. From The Bali House in Hawaii, to castles in England, villas in Morocco, and houseboats in Sausalito, get the inside scoop on the best in usually unique vacation rentals.

BRAINSTORMING: UNUSUALLY UNIQUE NICHE

Think about the following:

UNUSUALLY UNIQUE LOCATIONS: Identify if your property is located in an unusually unique area. Also identify unusually unique attractions, or if your home is unusually unique then, include the most unique attractions of your home in your brand. For example, is your home round-shaped, a house boat, near the UFO Watchtower or other unusual museums? Feature these as part of your brand.

UNUSUALLY UNIQUE ENTERPRISES: Seek out the unique local enterprises in the area, and include a pair of free or discounted tickets to these attractions when your guests book your home.

UNUSUALLY UNIQUE EVENTS: London Great Gorilla Run, Wisconsin's Annual Bar Stool Race, or the Fairy Forest Festival in Virginia are just a few examples of unique events. Tap into these events if they intersect with your brand to invite guests to book with you.

TRAVEL AGENCIES: Host an open house to showcase

BRAINSTORMING: UNUSUALLY UNIQUE NICHE

vacation homes to travel agencies & pay them a 5-15% commission for bookings.

WHAT DO YOU THINK?

___

___

___

___

___

___

___

Notes:

___

___

___

___

___

DON'T LET THEM STEAL YOUR BRAND

NICHE 8: VACATION RENTALS FOR THE SPORTS ENTHUSIAST

ARE YOU AN ATHLETIC PERSON WHO WANTS TO BE PHYSICALLY CHALLENGED? DO YOU VIEW VACATION TIME AS AN OPPORTUNITY TO DO THE SPORTS YOU LOVE?

Seeking a get-up-and-go experience where you are surrounded by sporting opportunities? Grab your fishing pole, golf clubs, skis, snowboard, surfboard, bike, or tennis racket, and go play! After your athletic feats, relax in the Jacuzzi at your beautiful vacation rental!

BRAINSTORMING: SPORTS ENTHUSIAST NICHE

Think about the following:

SPORTS ENTHUSIAST LOCATIONS: If your vacation rental is located in a sports area, such as where the Olympics are being held, or a winning team, or if it is close to an important golf course, then brand your vacation rental for the sports enthusiast.

SPORTS ENTHUSIAST ENTERPRISES: Network with local golf courses, resorts, ski lodges, and see about getting a discounted or fee day pass to include when your guess books your Sports niched vacation home.

SPORTS ENTHUSIAST EVENTS: Research every sporting event in your area. Then network, Invite them for private or open house tours of your rentals. Advertise your availably on a regularly. People need places to stay during major sporting tournaments.

TRAVEL AGENCIES: Host an open house to showcase vacation homes to travel agencies & pay them a 5-15% commission for bookings.

BRAINSTORMING: SPORTS ENTHUSIAST NICHE

WHAT DO YOU THINK?

Notes:

DON'T LET THEM STEAL YOUR BRAND

NICHE 9: VACATION RENTALS FOR WINE LOVERS

OENOLOGY HAS BEEN AN ART FOR CENTURIES. AN EXPLOSION OF VINEYARDS GLOBALLY HAS MADE A NICHE FOR THE WINE LOVERS.

Vacation rentals homes are available specifically for the wine connoisseur to enjoy beautiful scenery in and around vineyards. Tours and wine tastings are available in lovely places. You will discover the intriguing history of the vineyards and workers who lovingly tend the vines.

BRAINSTORMING: WINE LOVER NICHE

Think about the following:

WINE LOVERS LOCATIONS: If your vacation rental is located near wineries you could brand your vacation rental for the Wine Connoisseur. Network with these wineries, and include their wines.

WINE LOVERS ENTERPRISES: Connect with the wine shops, restaurants who specialize in high end wines to exchange promotional materials with those who book through a referral from them.

WINE LOVERS EVENTS: Check for the dates of wine tasting in the area, or any wine and food festivals. Offer a private tour, open house, exchange website links, or a discounted ticket to the event to those who book your Vacation Rental. Include wine books on your coffee table, wine openers, and such.

TRAVEL AGENCIES: Host an open house to showcase vacation homes to travel agencies & pay them a 5-15% commission for bookings.

BRAINSTORMING: WINE LOVER NICHE

WHAT DO YOU THINK?

_____

_____

_____

_____

_____

_____

Notes:

_____

_____

_____

_____

_____

_____

_____

DON'T LET THEM STEAL YOUR BRAND

NICHE 10: VALUE CONSCIOUS VACATION RENTALS

ON A BUDGET, BUT WANT TO ENJOY A MEMORABLE VACATION? IN THIS NICHE, VRTG UNVEILS SECRETS OF REASONABLY PRICED, HIGH-VALUE VACATION HOMES.

In these rentals you'll be sure to stretch your dollar and get great value and fun times for your money. Don't let the stress of money stop you from experiencing the vacation of a lifetime!

BRAINSTORMING: VALUE CONSCIOUS NICHE

Think about the following:

VALUE CONSCIOUS LOCATIONS: Your location will have inexpensive or free things to do. Find out what, when, and where these events are, and include this information in your branding literature.

VALUE CONSCIOUS ENTERPRISES: Locate bargain restaurants, grocery stores, public transportation, thrift stores and provide this info in your WELCOME MANUAL. Get coupons, discounts, and bargain shop hours as well.

VALUE CONSCIOUS EVENTS: Tap into antique and collectible shows, saving money workshops, budgeting and finance courses or trade shows, and offer a free day if they book 6 days to anyone who attends these events.

TRAVEL AGENCIES: Host an open house to showcase vacation homes to travel agencies & pay them a 5-15% commission for bookings.

BRAINSTORMING: VALUE CONSCIOUS NICHE

WHAT DO YOU THINK?

Notes:

DON'T LET THEM STEAL YOUR BRAND

NICHE 11: PET FRIENDLY VACATION RENTALS

PET FRIENDLY VACATION HOMES EXTEND THEIR HOSPITALITY TO INDOOR PETS WHO HAVE BECOME AN INVALUABLE MEMBER OF THEIR HOUSEHOLD.

Do you consider your pet a member of your family? Millions of pet owners do. This niche is highly relevant for people who will not leave their pets in a kennel, let alone hire a pet sitter. Moreover, many families would miss their pet, and expect their pet to enjoy vacation with them. As we explore this niche, you will discover that some tourist towns are even "pet-friendly," and make special allowances for "man's best friend."

BRAINSTORMING: PET FRIENDLY NICHE

Think about the following:

PET FRIENDLY LOCATIONS: Identify pet friendly areas, stores, and restaurants in your city. For example, Colorado Springs has a world-famous leash-free dog park. On the other hand, the San Diego beach area also has a leash-free beach.

PET FRIENDLY ENTERPRISES: Find local pet stores and see if you can co-market. For example, get discounts, coupons, and bargains for your guests. Perhaps exchange your flyer on their bulletin board as well.

PET FRIENDLY EVENTS: Connect with local kennels and pet associations and let them know you have a pet friendly vacation rental. Mark every pet show and pet friendly event around your vacation rental and advertise to your guests.

TRAVEL AGENCIES: Host an open house to showcase vacation homes to travel agencies & pay them a 5-15% commission for bookings.

BRAINSTORMING: PET FRIENDLY NICHE

WHAT DO YOU THINK?

_____

_____

_____

_____

_____

_____

Notes:

_____

_____

_____

_____

_____

_____

_____

DON'T LET THEM STEAL YOUR BRAND

NICHE 12: YOUR VACATION RENTAL NICHE

DEFINE THE NICHE MARKET THAT BEST SUITS THE TASTE, PERSONALITY, AND LOCATION OF YOUR VACATION RENTAL PROPERTIES. NICHE BRAND YOUR PROPERTY MANAGEMENT COMPANY OR INDIVIDUAL PROPERTIES.

Name Your Niche Here: _____

_____

Describe Your Niche: _____

_____

_____

_____

BRAINSTORMING: YOUR VACATION RENTAL NICHE

Now you are going to brainstorm your vacation rental niche. Just implementing one of these brilliant ideas could help you reach your number.

Think about the following:

YOUR VACATION RENTAL NICHE RELATED LOCATIONS:

_____

_____

_____

_____

_____

_____

BRAINSTORMING: YOUR VACATION RENTAL NICHE

YOUR VACATION RENTAL NICHE RELATED ENTERPRISES:

_____

_____

_____

_____

_____

_____

YOUR VACATION RENTAL NICHE RELATED EVENTS:

_____

_____

_____

_____

_____

_____

_____

DON'T LET THEM STEAL YOUR BRAND

Notes:

SUMMARY

1. Know who your traveler is and reach out to them in their area of interest.

2. Create a direct relationship with them using emails, social media, booking specials, referral and review incentives.

3. Push your niche through branded promotional materials and items.

4. Create independence from the big listing sites by offering guests who have stayed with you a way to rebook with you directly.

VACATION RENTAL AGENCIES
BOOK DIRECT & SAVE

In a monopoly-type power grab, many OTA's have recently stripped their listings of property brand and contact information.

Find Rentals, founded in 2002, operates on a different business model. In promoting ***professionally managed vacation rental properties***, they support guest and management relationships with transparency. Find Rentals builds property management brand and enhances the connection between hosts and guests.

Find Rentals has assisted millions of travelers in selecting stunning accommodations with professionally managed vacation rental agencies.

Attract more bookings by collaborating with a 300+ client network. The Find Rentals network positions your company by promoting your brand, destinations, events, activities, suitability, and superior hospitality to achieve lasting success in the vacation rental industry.

$36 PER PROPERTY PER YEAR
No Gimmicks. No Commissions. No Hidden Fees.
CALL 320.815.7669 OR EMAIL CINDY@FINDRENTALS.COM

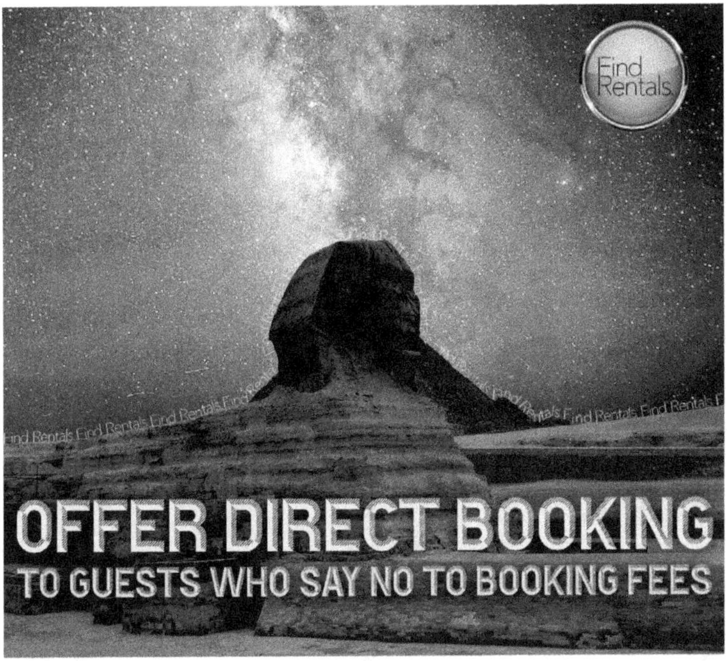
Find Rentals
OFFER DIRECT BOOKING
TO GUESTS WHO SAY NO TO BOOKING FEES

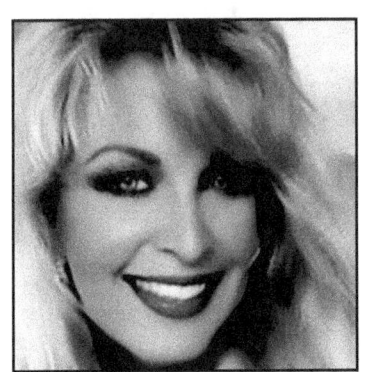

TO BOOK
DEBORAH S. NELSON
AS A SPEAKER

CONTACT: SARA WINNER
Publishing Coordinator
Phone Number: +1 (202) 871-8774
Email: findrentals@thevacationrentalguide.com

www.ingramcontent.com/pod-product-compliance
Lightning Source LLC
Chambersburg PA
CBHW050109230526
45470CB00004B/1740